Deschutes
Public Library

D07000€3

C. 1

COSTUME AROUND THE WORLD
China

Anne Rooney

CHELSEA CLUBHOUSE

An Imprint of Chelsea House Publishers

Copyright © 2008 Bailey Publishing Associates Ltd

Produced for Chelsea Clubhouse by Bailey Publishing Associates Ltd
11a Woodlands, Hove BN3 6TJ
England

Project Manager: Roberta Bailey
Editor: Alex Woolf
Text Designer: Jane Hawkins
Picture Research: Roberta Bailey and Shelley Noronha

All rights reserved. No part of this book may be reproduced or utilized in any form or by any means, electronic or mechanical, including photocopying, recording, or by any information storage or retrieval systems, without permission in writing from the publisher.
For information contact:

Chelsea Clubhouse
An imprint of Chelsea House Publishers
132 West 31st Street
New York NY 10001

ISBN 978-0-7910-9765-6

Library of Congress Cataloging-in-Publication Data
Costume around the world.—1st ed.
      v. cm.
    Includes bibliographical references and index.
    Contents: [1] China / Anne Rooney—[2] France / Kathy Elgin—[3] Germany / Cath Senker—[4] India / Kathy Elgin—[5] Italy / Kathy Elgin—[6] Japan / Jane Bingham—[7] Mexico / Jane Bingham—[8] Saudi Arabia / Cath Senker—[9] Spain / Kathy Elgin—[10] United States / Liz Gogerly.
    ISBN 978-0-7910-9765-6 (v. 1)—ISBN 978-0-7910-9766-3 (v. 2)—ISBN 978-0-7910-9767-0 (v. 3)—ISBN 978-0-7910-9768-7 (v. 4)—ISBN 978-0-7910-9769-4 (v. 5)—ISBN 978-0-7910-9770-0 (v. 6)—ISBN 978-0-7910-9771-7 (v. 7)—ISBN 978-0-7910-9773-1 (v. 8)— ISBN 978-0-7910-9772-4 (v. 9)—ISBN 978-0-7910-9774-8 (v. 10) 1. Clothing and dress—Juvenile literature.
    GT518.C67 2008
    391—dc22   2007042756

Chelsea Clubhouse books are available at special discounts when purchased in bulk quantities for businesses, associations, institutions, or sales promotions. Please call our Special Sales Department in New York at (212) 967-8800 or (800) 322-8755.

You can find Chelsea Clubhouse on the World Wide Web at: http://www.chelseahouse.com

Printed and bound in Hong Kong

10 9 8 7 6 5 4 3 2 1

The publishers would like to thank the following for permission to reproduce their pictures:
AP/Kyodo: 24.
Bailey Publishing Associates Ltd: 11.
Chris Fairclough Worldwide Ltd: 4 (Adrian Cooper), 12 (Adrian Cooper), 21(Adrian Cooper), 23.
Jupiter Images/Image State: 14, 22.
Topfoto: 15, 20 (Houghton), 25 (Linda Rich), 26, 27, 29.
Topfoto/Fratelli Alinari Museum of the History of Photography: 7, 13, 24.
Topfoto/RSC/Alinari Archives Management: 9, 10, 18, 19.
Topfoto/The Image Works: 8, 16 and title page, 28.
Werner Forman Archive: 6.
Xinhua/Landov: 17.

Contents

China and Its Costumes

China is geographically the third-largest country in the world after Russia and Canada. The terrain ranges from plains to mountains, from barren deserts to waterlogged lowlands. The people of China have different clothing to suit the places where they live and their local weather.

There are many different groups of people living in China, and they wear a rich variety of traditional costumes. Like people everywhere, they have also developed clothes for different purposes, with costumes for special occasions, for work, leisure, and other activities.

Costume through the ages

China is one of the oldest civilizations in the world, with a recorded history of

Schoolgirls in Guizhou Province wear traditional local dress every day.

over 3,000 years. For much of that time, it was ruled by wealthy emperors who exercised immense power. Often, they laid down rules about what people could wear. The peasants who worked the land could barely afford clothes, but their rulers wore extravagant silk costumes, richly decorated with embroidery.

For many centuries, China cut itself off from the rest of the world. In recent years, though, many Chinese people have begun to wear the clothes common in the West. Many regional costumes still survive, and people often wear traditional Chinese dress for special occasions.

For thousands of years, rich people and poor people in China dressed very differently, reflecting their different lives.

Furs and fabric

Traditional Chinese costume is based on Manchu clothing, made from animal skins. The Manchus were a people who originated in northeast China and ruled the country between 1636 and 1912. They used one animal pelt for the back and two for the front of their garment. When the Chinese started to use cloth, they wove long narrow strips. They used one strip for each side of the body, folding it over the shoulder and stitching the strips together at the back.

Thousands of Years of Costume

For thousands of years, China was an empire. When one dynasty was overthrown, another one took its place. The earliest records of Chinese costume date from the Han dynasty (206 BCE–220 CE).

Robes and rags

The emperors, their families, and the people in their courts wore fabulous, ornate clothes made of silk and fur. The poor peasants often wore rags or made clothes from materials such as straw and other plant fibers.

Men and women of the imperial court wore long silk "dragon robes," with an opening down the front and a flap that folded over to one side. Men's robes were split at the back and front to make horseback riding easier.

The design of a dragon robe shows elements of the earth—waves and mountains—at the bottom and of the sky or heavens near the top. Here a bird represents the sky.

Dragon robes for winter were quilted or lined with fur. Summer robes were made of thin silk. The emperor set the date and hour when everyone had to change from winter to summer clothes.

End of empire

The last Chinese emperor was overthrown in 1912, and a republic was established. The traditional distinctions between ranks were overturned. In 1949, the Communist revolution brought another change. Again, costume was governed by law. But this time, everyone had to wear the same outfit of pants and a jacket.

Only one hundred years ago, wealthy Chinese people still wore ornate clothes.

Sumptuary laws

The emperors made rules, called sumptuary laws, about the colors and designs to be worn by people of different ranks. In 1759, Emperor Qianlong ruled that only an emperor could wear bright yellow and only his family could wear robes decorated with five-clawed dragons. Officials had four-clawed dragons. High-ranking officials had a robe with nine dragons, eight visible and one hidden on the inside.

Hot and Cold, Wet and Dry

Some parts of northern China have snow all year and no summer, but in the south there is no winter. Monsoon rains drench some areas, while others are parched deserts. The varied climate has affected how people dress.

Mongolian people wear a tunic called a *del* with long sleeves that can be turned down over the hands to protect them from cold.

Sun and snow

Temperatures in China range from -18 °F (-28 °C) in the northern winter to 86 °F (30 °C) during summer in the south. In the coldest areas, people wear quilted clothes, with a layer of cotton or wool padding between two layers of fabric.

People have always used furs to line their clothes and make warm hats and

boots. The furs of dogs, goats, sheep, cats, foxes, and raccoons are used in different areas. In some places, even exotic furs from endangered species have been worn, including tiger, lynx, and snow leopard. In the past, poor people sometimes stuffed paper inside their clothes to keep warm.

Men attending a festival in Labrang, Gansu, in northwest China, wear hats made from rare furs.

In the hottest places, people wear thin clothes of cotton or other plant fibers. The rich used to wear very fine silk in summer.

Wet weather

In the south, there can be 80 inches (200 centimeters) of rain a year. Rain-resistant clothes can be made from gummed silk, a waterproof fabric made by treating silk with plant extracts and mud, and finally varnishing it. Peasants used to weave rain capes from grass and straw.

The coolie hat

People who work in the countryside often wear a coolie hat to protect them from the sun and the rain. It is a shallow cone-shaped hat made of woven straw or sedge over a framework of bamboo. A circular band holds it on the head, and a strap under the chin keeps the hat in place.

Culture and Cultural Revolution

Cultural change has had a big impact on Chinese costume. Chinese people have been told what to wear first by their emperors and, later, by Communist rulers. Today, at last, they can wear what they like, but some people, such as monks and nuns, choose a way of life that requires special clothing.

Buddhist monks wear plain, simple robes, but they have ornate crowns for a religious ceremony.

Monks in rags

There are many Buddhists in China. Buddhist monks wear simple robes intended to show their poverty. Traditionally, their robes are patched together from rags. Some monks tear their robes

and stitch them together again, or leave holes in them. They are often brown, gray, or blue, although monks in Tibet (in southwest China) wear red robes.

The Buddhist robe is perhaps the oldest style of costume in the world, having remained much the same for 2,500 years.

Communist clothes

In 1966, Chinese leader Mao Zedong led the Cultural Revolution, which aimed to remove social differences between people. Ornate clothes were banned, and everyone had to wear identical clothes: a simple cotton work suit made up of a jacket and loose pants. In the West, this became known as the Mao suit. It was blue, gray, or dark green. The jacket was loose and straight, with a small collar and four pockets.

Since the death of Mao in 1976, most Chinese people in cities have begun to wear Western-style casual clothes and business suits.

The Mao suit made everyone look the same. It was comfortable and functional, too.

Origins of the Mao suit

The suit was first introduced by the early republican leader Sun Zhongshan and is properly called a Zhongshan suit. It was based on the clothing worn by Chinese men in Japan. It was later given a turned-down collar and four pockets. The suit was first worn by officials and, later, by everyone.

Fabrics and Fibers

The Chinese have used plant fibers, silk, and furs for many centuries. In modern China, synthetic fabrics are now available and everyone can afford warm clothing.

Silk

Chinese people have made silk for 5,000 years. It is a very fine, light, strong, and warm fiber, made from the cocoons spun by silkworms. The cocoons are baked, killing the grubs inside, and the cocoon is unwound. Each silkworm can produce a thread up to 0.6 mile (1 kilometer) long.

Secret silk

For centuries, all silk came from China. The Chinese were very protective of their silk industry and did not allow anyone to take silkworms out of the country. According to legend, silkworms were smuggled out of China to Byzantium (now Turkey) in about 550 CE by two monks, who hid them inside hollow canes. The Byzantines, in turn, jealously guarded the secret of silk.

This man works in a Chinese palace open to tourists. He wears a traditional court costume from the past.

Plant fibers

Plants such as hemp, ramie (China grass), and cotton provide fibers that are spun into thread and woven into cloth. Hemp and ramie were used in China for many years to make heavy, strong cloth.

Poor people in the countryside often used rice straw to weave clothes, sandals, and hats. They sometimes used tree bark or bamboo to make shoes and protective clothing.

Animal furs and wool

People in the colder regions traditionally hunted animals for furs. Wool from goats and sheep can be spun into yarn and woven into fabric too, although the Chinese have never used much wool. Cashmere, a very fine wool from goats, is made into a light, warm cloth in Inner Mongolia (in northeast China).

Rice straw overcoats helped to protect people from the rain and were cheap and easy to make.

Tribes and Traditions

China is made up of many tribes and national groups, including 56 different ethnic groups. Many of these have their own traditional costumes. Even though many people wear Western-style dress much of the time, they wear their traditional costumes for special occasions, especially in remote villages.

Chinese dresses

The Han Chinese make up 92 percent of the population of China, and so for the vast majority, Han and Chinese traditional costume mean the same thing. Han traditional costume is made up of a jacket or dress with a small, upright collar, called a mandarin collar, and a side fastening with a flap that folds over the chest.

This woman from Dali in Yunnan Province wears her traditional tribal costume.

Rural dress

Among the many rural styles of costume, some are very colorful. Colors often have meanings in Chinese tradition. In Tibet, many people wear white or navy blue. White symbolizes purity and good fortune, and blue is worn to show respect for lakes and rivers.

In Inner Mongolia, people wear a loose, belted tunic with long sleeves and a side fastening. Most people ride horses, so the skirts of the tunic are slit to make this easy.

Animal symbols

Traditional Chinese costumes are often richly decorated with colorful embroidery or appliqué. Both colors and designs often have special meanings for the people who wear them. Animal designs are common. The crane is a symbol of long life, a phoenix brings good luck, and a horse represents endurance and loyalty. A tiger is believed to keep away harm and is commonly used on children's clothes.

The short belted tunic, split at the sides, and the long leather boots are excellent clothes for these horse-riding nomads in Mongolia.

Special Occasions

In most countries, people wear special clothes for occasions such as weddings and funerals or other events that mark changes in their lives.

Marriage costumes

Traditional Chinese brides wear a beautifully embroidered red jacket and skirt, often decorated with phoenix and dragon designs, and red shoes. For Chinese people, red is a symbol of happiness. A bride may wear a red veil or a headdress with a row of beads or tassels that hang like a curtain in front of her face. The wedding outfit sometimes includes a small mirror to protect the bride from evil influences.

The traditional bridegroom wears a long gown, a short jacket, red shoes, and a red silk sash over his shoulder. The sash is later used as a

A newly married couple in Beijing wear traditional wedding robes. The bride's robe has a phoenix design, a symbol of happiness.

16

baby carrier. As part of the ceremony, the groom's father places a cap decorated with cypress leaves on the groom's head.

In mourning

The usual color for funeral clothes is white, the Chinese color for sorrow. Mourning clothes used to be made from hemp, which is cheap enough to throw away after mourning. Hemp is still worn in some areas. In the cities, many people today wear a black gauze armband as a symbol of mourning. Female guests may wear white cloth flowers to a funeral.

Burial clothes

When they reach the age of 60, many people start to plan their funeral and choose clothes to be buried in. They wear two more garments on the upper body than on the lower body and never wear fur because they fear they may be reincarnated as an animal. Women are often buried in their wedding headdress or a cardboard copy of it.

To celebrate the Moon Festival in October, people may wear the traditional Han dynasty costume. This is a long robe like a kimono that folds over at the front and is worn with a sash around the waist.

How Men Dress Up

For business and special occasions, men in Chinese cities often wear Western suits. But for some occasions, it is still common to wear traditional Chinese dress.

Suits and gowns

For formal wear, Chinese men sometimes wear traditional Qing clothing, worn during the Qing dynasty (1644–1911). This consists of a long, straight gown with an upright collar and side fastening called a *chang pao*. It is usually dark blue or gray. It can be worn under a short black jacket called a *magua*, with very long, loose sleeves. Sometimes the sleeves are used to carry things—even small dogs. The cuffs may be turned back to show a lining of a different color.

For much of the 20th century, the Mao suit was formal wear for men.

Another formal style is the mandarin suit: a jacket with a small, upright collar worn over loose-fitting pants. The jacket usually fastens with seven toggles or fabric knots called frogs. Odd numbers are considered masculine and lucky.

In the countryside

Men in rural areas often wear a dark blue or gray gown or coat with a flap and side fastening, belted with a sash. The fabric is chosen to suit the climate and the man's wealth. It may be cotton, hemp, or silk. Old men in rural areas sometimes still wear the Mao suit for formal events.

This man in northwest China wears the traditional local costume at a festival.

Special headgear

In some regions, men wear very ornate hats or headdresses as part of their formal clothing. Men from the Bai group in Yunnan Province wear richly embroidered and decorated caps adorned with beads and buttons. In the cold Altai Mountains, Kazak men wear hats made from sheepskin and silk. The style varies from one village to another.

How Women Dress Up

For formal events, many Chinese women wear a *qipao*, a close-fitting dress with an upright collar based on the traditional costume of the Han Chinese. An alternative is a short jacket over a long skirt.

Qipao

The *qipao* is usually made from silk brocade that has a pattern woven into it. It usually has short, cap sleeves and may have a knee- or ankle-length skirt. The *qipao* is fitted closely to the body and is slit at the sides to make walking easier. It has a side fastening, with a flap folding over the top of the bodice from the center of the collar to the right armpit.

Modern interpretations of traditional Chinese dresses are on sale in China and in Chinese communities throughout the world.

Skirts

In some areas of China, women wear a skirt and blouse, gown, or jacket over pants or leggings. The traditional skirt has straight panels at the front and back and pleated panels at the sides to aid movement. The panels are attached to a wide waistband of a different fabric. The skirt is usually dark blue or black. The jacket, with an upright collar and front fastening, may be bright red or embroidered.

In some regions, a lavishly embroidered or decorated apron, ornate jewelry, and sometimes a complex headdress may also be part of a woman's formal wear.

Miao women in Guizhou Province wear their traditional headdresses and costumes.

Water buffalo headdress

Miao women from southwest China wear unusual headdresses for special occasions. Women from one village make a huge bundle of twisted hair and thread, using up to 10 pounds (4.5 kilograms) of their own hair and hair from their mothers and grandmothers. This is wrapped and tied in a figure-eight shape to look like the head of a water buffalo.

Mao Suits and Work Wear

For much of the 20th century, all Chinese people wore Mao suits for work. Today there is more variety. Many people wear informal clothes similar to those worn in the West, but in the countryside, these are often mixed with traditional Chinese styles.

This fisherman is wearing a traditional coolie hat and Mao-style jacket to work on his boat.

Peasants and farmers

People working in the countryside were very poor for many centuries. Their simple work costumes consisted of a collarless shirt or vest and pants that wrapped around the

Homemade work shoes

People in the countryside have always made shoes from woven grass or straw. These shoes often have plaited soles and may be shaped like slippers or flip-flops. Sometimes they are tied onto the feet around the ankle or have loops for the toes. Today many people wear inexpensive fabric shoes with plastic soles. Clogs carved from a piece of wood and with an upper of leather, rubber, or plastic are often worn in fish markets and other wet workplaces.

A soldier in dress uniform guards the Forbidden City in Beijing. For battle, he would not wear braided trousers and jacket or white gloves.

waist with no fastening. Some used grasses and straw to make their own clothing.

Business dress

Office workers in cities often wear Western pants or skirts and shirts to work. Even so, few men wear a jacket and tie every day. Except for very formal events, they are more likely to wear pants and a shirt or possibly a shirt, pants, and a jacket but no tie.

Military uniforms

Chinese soldiers wear an olive green uniform with the red star—the symbol of Communist China—on the two points of the collar and on the cap. For cold weather, soldiers wear a heavy overcoat of the same color and a fur hat with earflaps that can be folded down.

Time Off

Chinese people enjoy celebrating at dramatic festivals and carnivals. These provide a chance to make spectacular costumes for some of the traditional dances and parades and for onlookers to wear their best clothes.

Lion costumes

The lion dance is a traditional dance performed by one or two dancers who dress as a lion. When there are two dancers, one wears the head of the lion and the other the body. The costume is brightly colored

Colorful and elaborate costumes are used in this lion dance.

Chinese opera

Chinese opera has a long tradition. The ornate costumes are based on exaggerated versions of the clothes worn during periods of China's imperial history. The singers' faces are transformed with makeup and their hair is sculpted and decorated with a symbolic headdress. The costumes, headdresses, and face designs are traditional and give information about the rank and type of each character.

A character in the Guangzhou Opera.

and extravagant, with a large, fearsome-looking head. It is made of paper and fabric with a framework that may be bamboo, wood, metal, or plastic. In southern China, the dance is traditionally performed to bring luck and ward off evil.

Martial arts

People practicing martial arts—traditional Chinese combative sports—wear loose pants to the mid-calf and a loose jacket that overlaps at the front and ties with a sash. The costume allows easy movement and is made of hemp or thick cotton.

Tai chi chuan is a more gentle form of exercise involving slow, balanced movements. Many older people practice tai chi in Chinese parks in the early mornings and evenings. They wear loose clothes, which make it easy to move.

Underwear and Extra Wear

The tradition of decorating clothing with designs and colors that have meanings extends to underwear, hats, and shoes. Children's clothes in particular use symbolic animals to help protect the child.

These tiny embroidered silk shoes for bound feet were made in 1870.

Women's underwear

The belly band, or *dudou*, is a panel of fabric that covers the front of the body and fastens at the neck and back, somewhat like a short apron. Traditionally, it was decorated with embroidered symbols to ward off bad luck or to bring love and good fortune. Today some pregnant women wear a

Foot binding

For centuries, Chinese women were disabled by the cruel practice of foot-binding. The feet were bent over in early childhood and tightly bound with fabric so that they never grew beyond around 5 inches (13 centimeters) in length. Foot-binding stopped in the 1930s, but some elderly women still have bound feet. Beautifully decorated shoes for bound feet were a traditional part of women's dress.

belly band made of fabric designed to prevent the passage of radiation from mobile phones and other electronic equipment, which they fear may damage their growing baby.

Special clothes for children

Children's hats and shoes are often decorated with—or even made to look like—animals such as lions, tigers, and dragons to frighten away evil spirits. Their clothes may also be decorated with bells for the same reason. Some children wear a padlock charm to lock them to the earth, and others wear a collar like a dog to fool spirits into thinking they are animals. Until they are toilet trained, toddlers wear divided pants, split under the crotch, which allow them to squat when they need the toilet.

This tiger hat from northern China has two tiger faces, intended to protect the child.

China in the World

Thousands of years ago, China began exporting silk to other countries. Now it exports clothing in many fabrics, including synthetic fibers. At the same time, China has adopted many Western fashions.

Clothing for the world

Wages are still low in China, so clothes can be made cheaply there. Many Western clothing companies have their own designs manufactured in large Chinese factories.

These women are working in a garment factory in Shenzhen, Guangdong Province.

People who have left China and set up Chinese communities in other countries have taken their fashions with them. Some traditional Chinese fashions have become very popular outside China. It is easy to buy Chinese clothes such as *qipao*, embroidered Chinese dressing gowns, and mandarin jackets in the West. The flat, black fabric shoes with plastic or straw soles worn by many Chinese people are also cheap and popular.

Chinese silk has a global reputation for its high quality. It is sold throughout the world as fabric as well as being made into clothes for sale abroad.

Western clothes

Like many other countries that have grown quickly in recent years, China has adopted many aspects of Western culture. Most people in cities wear Western-style dress for everyday activities. Even in the countryside, many people mix Western styles with traditional elements. In particular, T-shirts and blouses are common work wear, often worn with Chinese-style pants.

Online tailors

Hong Kong tailors have been popular with visitors for a long time. They will tailor suits, dresses, and other clothes very quickly at reasonable prices and to a high standard. Some are now taking advantage of the Internet to make clothes for people outside China. Traveling fitters measure customers in the United States and Europe, and customers choose designs and order online.

Clothes in many Western styles are made in China. They are sold in China and exported to other countries.

Glossary

appliqué A decoration on cloth, created by sewing on patches of different fabric to make a design.

bodice The part of a dress that covers the upper part of the body and to which the skirt and sleeves are attached.

brocade A fabric with a raised design, created in the weaving process.

Buddhists People who follow the teachings of the Buddha, a spiritual leader who died around 500 BCE.

cap sleeves Little sleeves that look like a cap over the shoulder.

Communist revolution The uprising in 1949 in which the government of China was overthrown and the Communist government was established.

Cultural Revolution A movement led by the Chinese leader Mao Zedong to suppress intellectuals and remove all relics of non-Communist culture. It lasted from 1966 to 1976.

embroidery A decoration on cloth created by making pictures or patterns from stitching, often in different colors.

empire A group of territories, nations, or peoples ruled by a single authority.

frog A decorative fastening for the front of a garment, consisting of a knot or toggle and a loop of fabric.

gauze Very fine, thin fabric.

hemp Thick fabric made from the fibers of the hemp plant.

monsoon The season of very heavy rain, lasting several weeks or months.

phoenix A mythological bird resembling an eagle that lives for 500 years, then burns to death on a pyre from whose ashes another phoenix rises.

qipao A style of Han Chinese dress made up of a close-fitting robe with a side fastening and a small, upright collar.

ramie A flowering plant of the nettle family, used to make fabric.

reincarnated Reborn in another body after death. This refers to the belief held by some traditions that when the body dies, the soul can return to the earth to live another life in a different body.

republic A system of government based on the consent of the people. Often the rulers are democratically elected.

sedge A type of grass.

sumptuary laws Laws that regulate the clothing that people can wear.

synthetic fabric Fabric made chemically, not from plant or animal fibers. Most synthetic fabrics are derived from petrochemicals.

tai chi chuan A martial art consisting of disciplined, slow movements.

tailor A person who makes clothes that are fitted to the measurements of an individual.

terrain The physical features and character of an area of land.

toggle A fastening consisting of a bead or knot, which is usually secured with a loop of fabric, thread, or leather.

Further Information

Books

Goh, Sui Noi, and Lim, Bee Ling. *Welcome to My Country: China.* Gareth Stevens, 1999.

Lynch, Emma. *We're from China.* Heinemann Library, 2005.

Sebag-Montefiore, Hugh. *Eyewitness Books: China.* Dorling Kindersley, 2007.

Waterlow, Julia. *We Come from China.* Raintree, 2000.

Waterlow, Julia. *Letters from Around the World: China.* Cherrytree Books, 2005.

Web sites

udel.edu/~orzada/china1.htm
Information on traditional Chinese costume.

asianart.com/textiles/textile.html
A Web site all about Chinese textiles.

www.chinesefolkculture.com/info_view.asp?ID=1356&ArticlePage=1
Information on Qing-style clothing.

www3.uakron.edu/worldciv/russ/minority.html
Photos of costumes worn by minority ethnic groups in China.

www.bookrags.com/research/clothing-traditionalhong-kong-ema-02/
A Web site on traditional clothing in Hong Kong.

Index